A postcard for you
to color and mail.

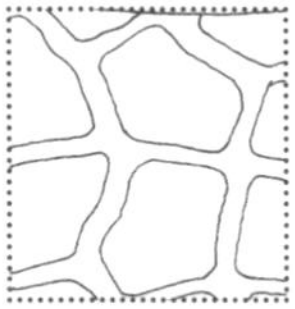

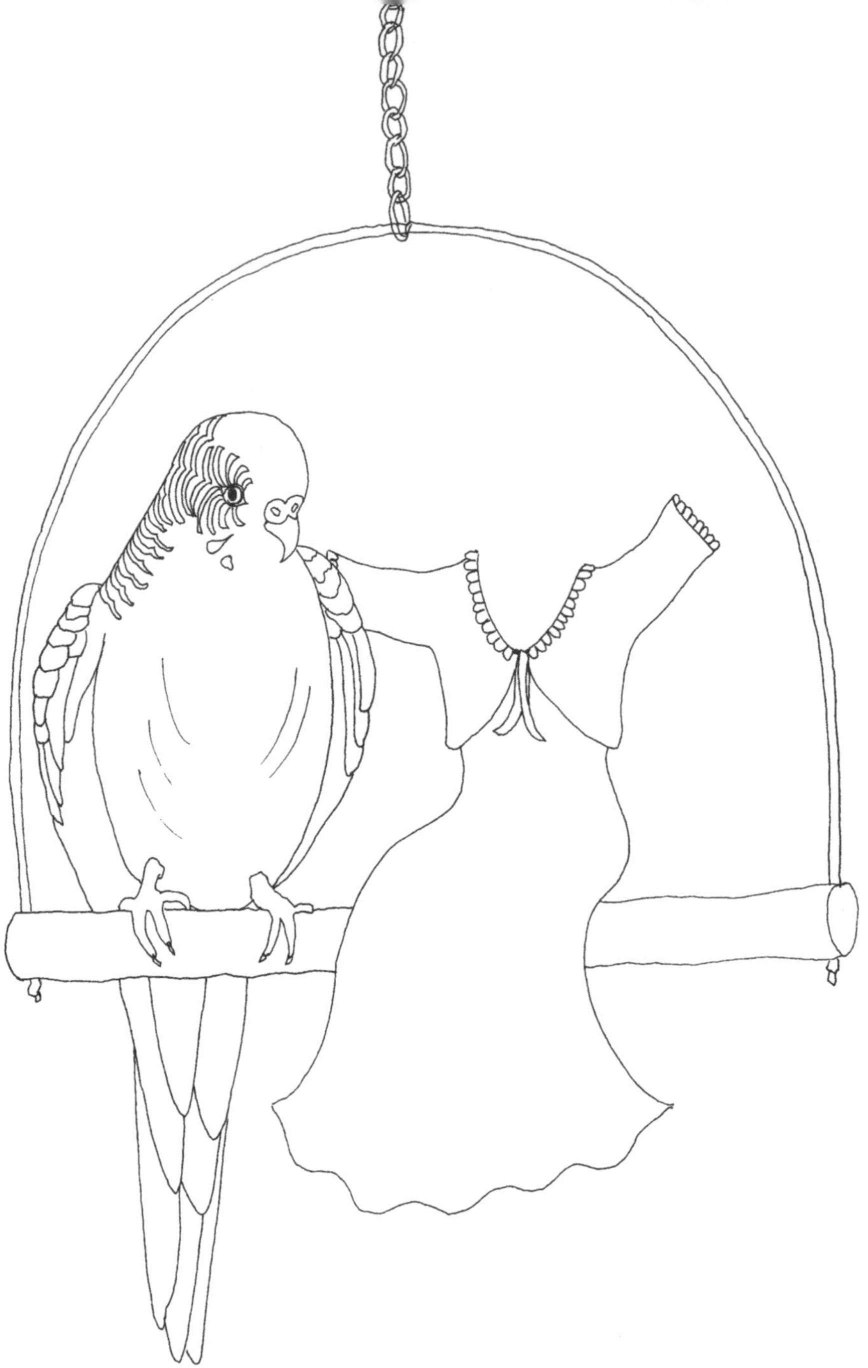

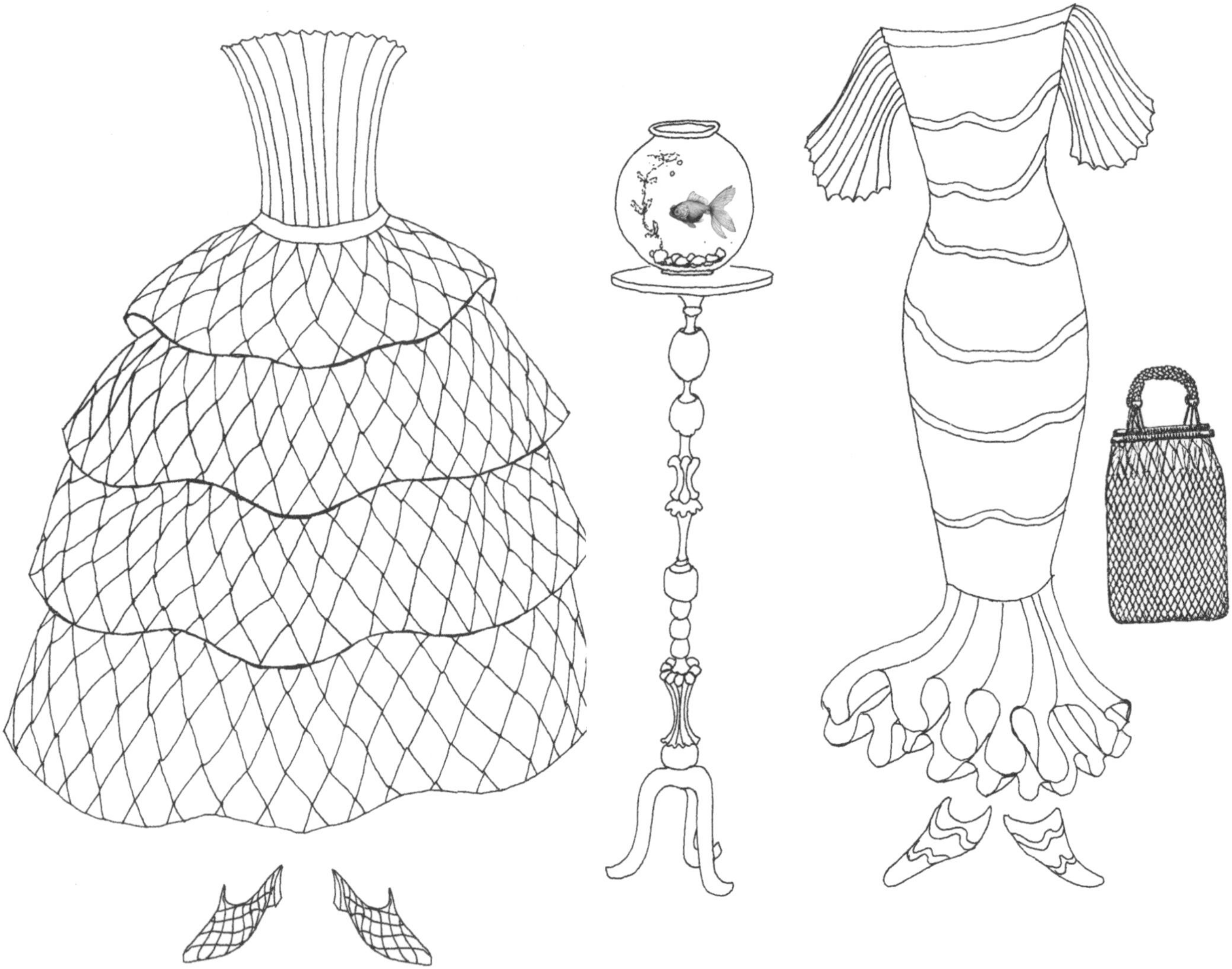

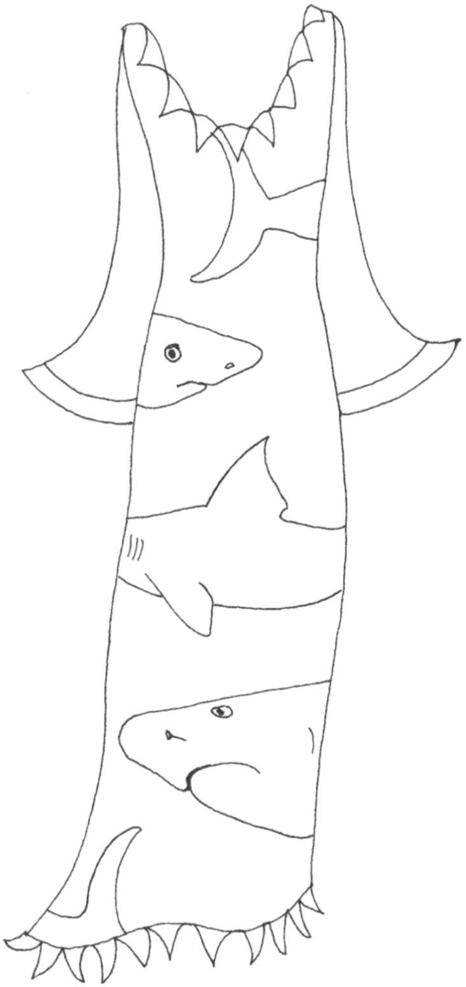

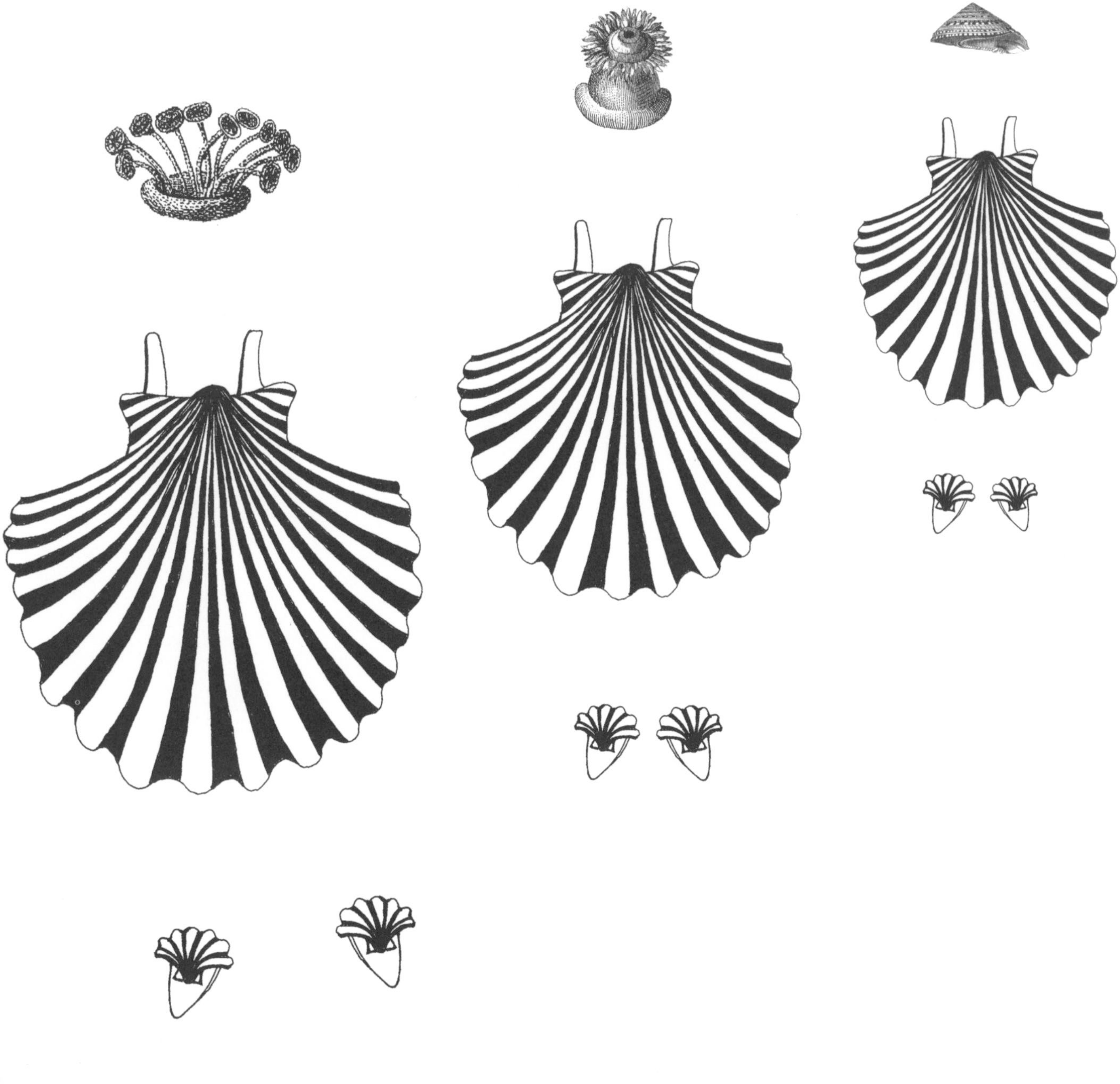

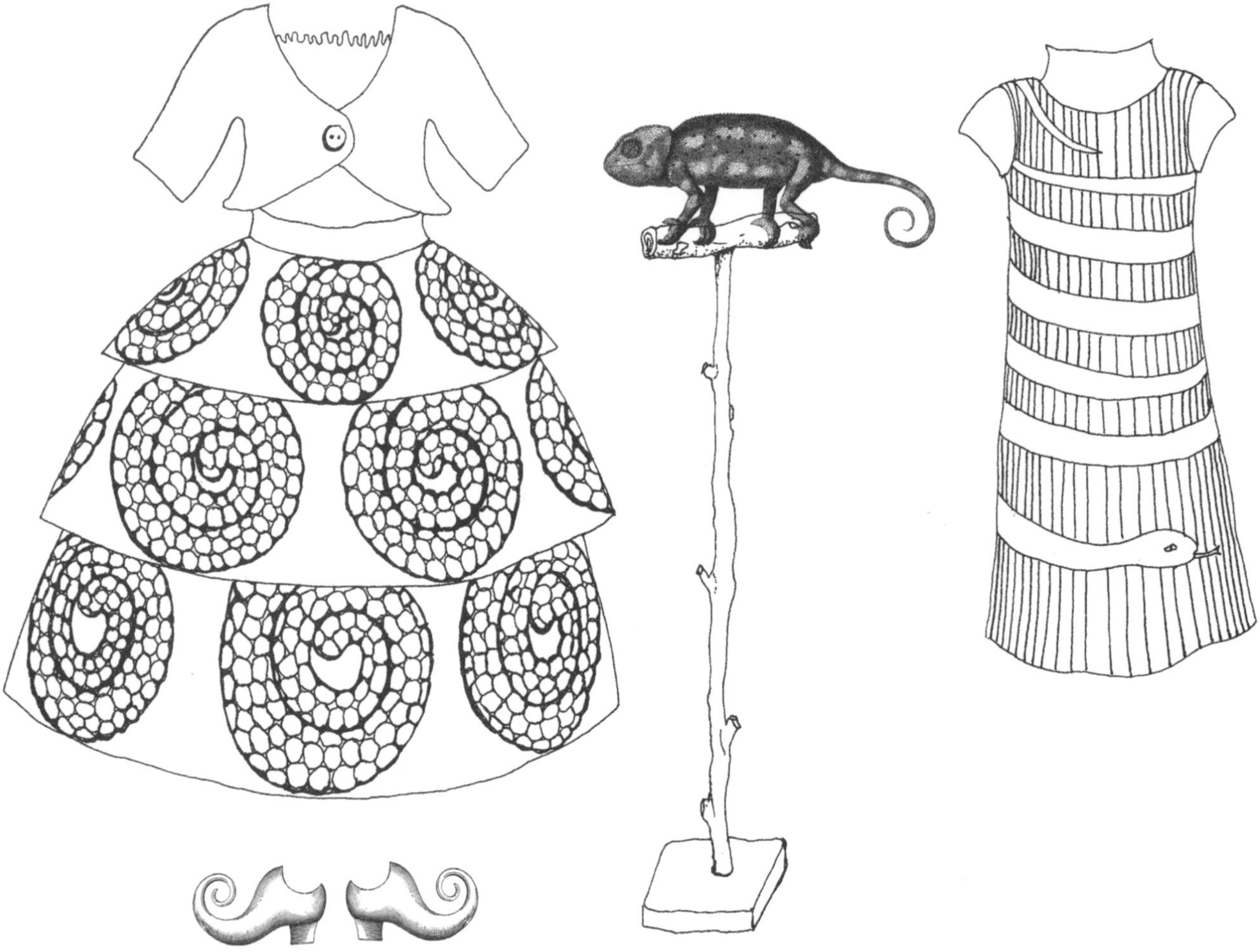

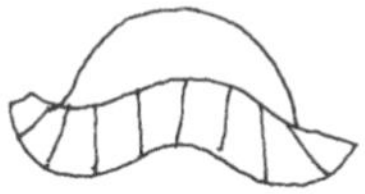

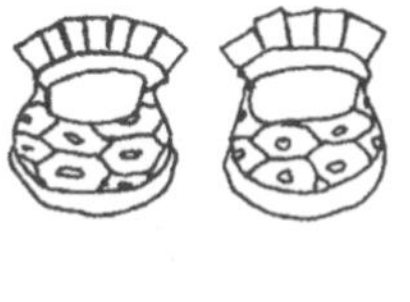

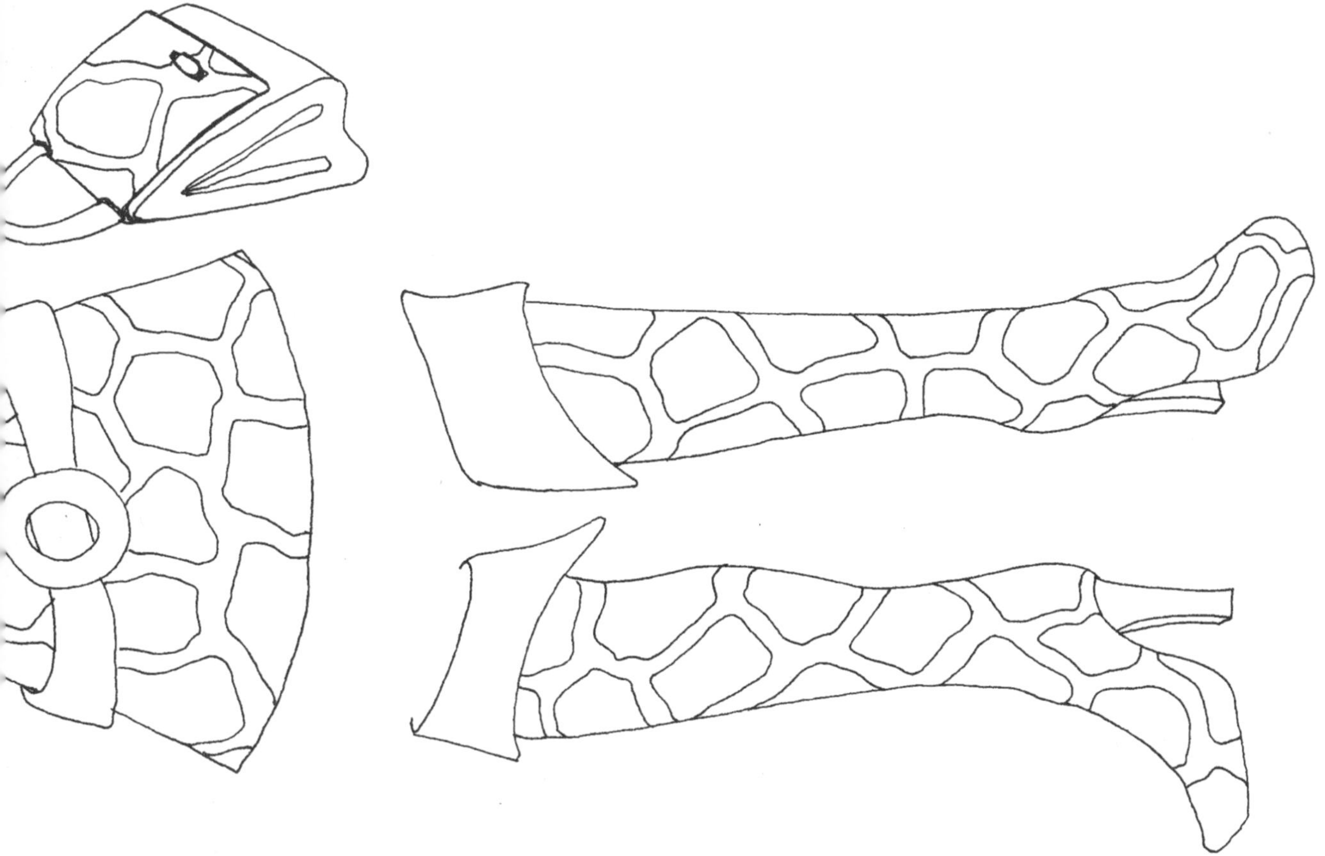

LAVENDER WATER

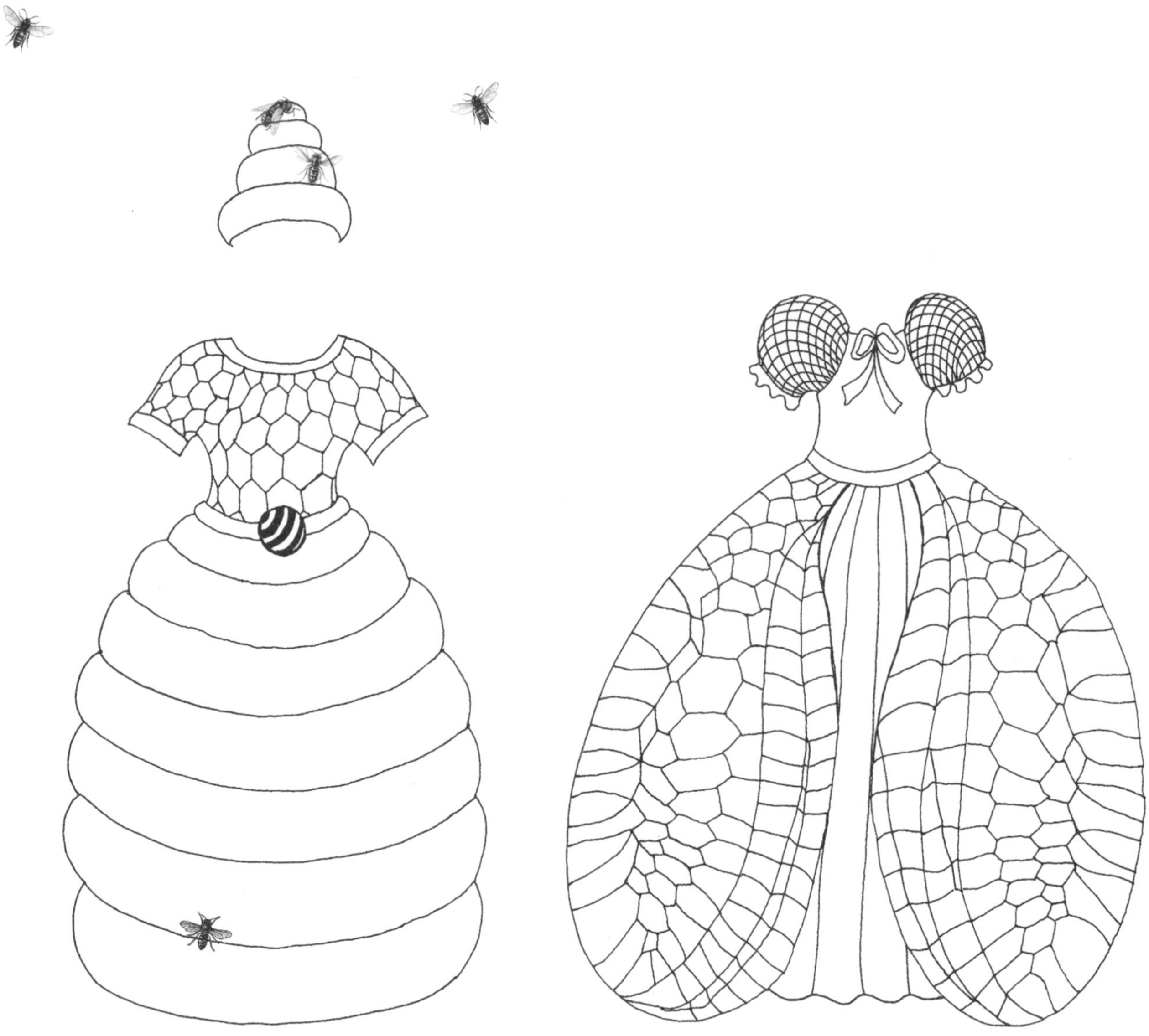

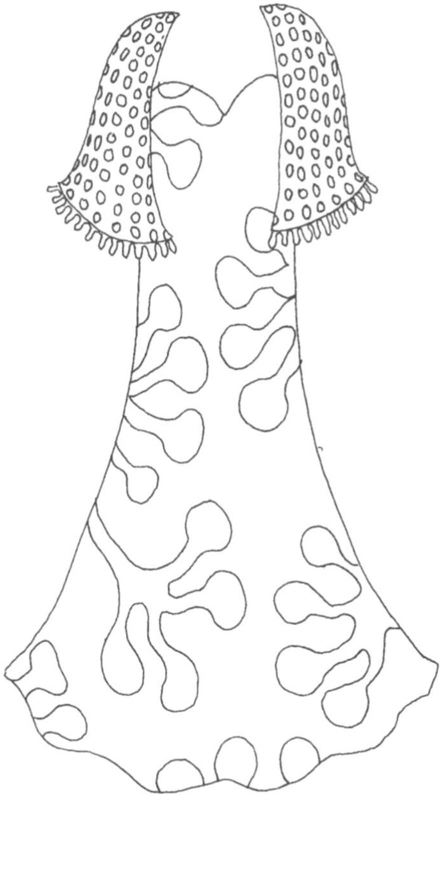

Another postcard for
you to color and mail.

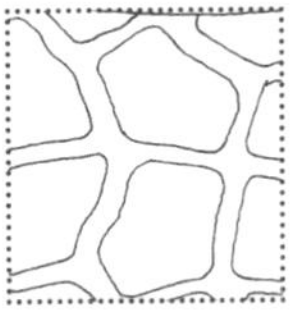